CHRISTOPHER

A German Life

drawn from interviews with

BRUNHILDE POMSEL
(1911–2017)

Christopher Hampton's play is drawn from
the testimony Pomsel gave when she finally
broke her silence in the documentary film
A German Life to filmmakers Christian Krönes,
Olaf Müller, Roland Schrotthofer and Florian
Weigensamer, produced by Blackbox Film

FABER & FABER

First published in 2019
by Faber and Faber Limited
74–77 Great Russell Street, London WC1B 3DA

Typeset by Country Setting, Kingsdown, Kent CT14 8ES
Printed and bound in the UK by CPI Group (UK) Ltd,
Croydon CR0 4YY

A CIP record for this book
is available from the British Library

ISBN 978-0-571-35617-1

2 4 6 8 10 9 7 5 3 1

A German Life

Christopher Hampton was born in the Azores in 1946. He wrote his first play, *When Did You Last See My Mother?*, at the age of eighteen. Since then, his plays have included *The Philanthropist*, *Savages*, *Tales from Hollywood*, *Les Liaisons Dangereuses*, *White Chameleon*, *The Talking Cure* and *Appomattox*. He has translated plays by Ibsen, Molière, von Horváth, Chekhov, Yasmina Reza and Florian Zeller. His television work includes adaptations of *The History Man* and *Hôtel du Lac*. His screenplays include *The Honorary Consul*, *The Good Father*, *Dangerous Liaisons*, *Mary Reilly*, *Total Eclipse*, *The Quiet American*, *Atonement*, *Cheri*, *A Dangerous Method*, *Carrington*, *The Secret Agent* and *Imagining Argentina*, the last three of which he also directed.

Author's Note

I first became aware of Brunhilde Pomsel when Jonathan Kent introduced me to the documentary film *Ein Deustsches Leben*, directed by the Viennese collective, Christian Krönes, Florian Weigensamer, Roland Schrotthofer and Olaf S. Müller. Presented in an aesthetically beautiful black-and-white format, shot to highlight a 102-year-old face craggier than W. H. Auden's, interspersed with clips from contemporary films and images from the death-camps, it leaves an impressively sombre aftertaste, but not necessarily an easy route for a dramatist to follow. Nor was the book based on the film (called in English *The Work I Did*) very suggestive in this respect. So, fascinated as I was by Ms Pomsel, I was more or less at a loss as to how to proceed, when Christian Krönes gave me the 235-page transcript of the conversations he and his team had held with her in 2013.

Suddenly she came vividly to life: her liveliness, her humour, her descriptive powers and her evasiveness, often signalled by a fracturing of her normal easy fluency. Whereas, after watching the film, it's scarcely possible to believe her claims that she knew nothing of the Final Solution, even though she was working in Goebbels's office, I found myself half-convinced by the transcript, particularly her majestic indifference to what might be happening in the outside world. Anxious to think well of everyone – anyone not described as *sehr nett* (very nice) is clearly a complete bastard – proud of how *pflichtbewusst* (conscientious) she was in her work and properly sceptical of the bizarre and irrational imperatives of politics and men (which she regards as synonymous), she belongs to that constituency so familiar to us today: the person who thinks well of the authorities. The irony is that it was precisely the office in which she found herself working – Goebbels's Propaganda Ministry– that invented and perfected the techniques, so cynically used by today's politicians to mislead, exploit and blatantly lie to people very like herself.

To put it simply, I have no idea to what extent she is telling the truth; and it was this central ambiguity that finally most attracted me to the subject. In general, I've always preferred to leave judgements and conclusions to the audience: the case of Brunhilde Pomsel seems to me particularly finely poised.

*

This is the first time I've written a one-person show. Writing for actors, which is how I usually describe my profession, is an essentially collaborative process, and writing for one actor all the more so. Those of you who have watched the play would not have to be especially eagle-eyed to notice a good many differences between text and performance. In particular, the text is around twenty per cent longer than the performance script. If you're lucky enough to be working with the incomparable Maggie Smith, you're well-advised to pay close attention to her suggestions and instincts and to do everything you can to play to her many strengths. I think of this piece therefore as raw material, through which any future performer can carve their own passage.

At the Royal Court Theatre, where I began my career, the text was held to be sacred, fierce battles were fought over commas, and any thought of asking a writer to 'develop' his or her script would have been regarded as a heresy and contemptuously dismissed. I'm still marked by that training; I prefer, on the whole, for my plays to be performed as written – but I must admit that the process of deconstruction, analysis and distillation undertaken with Maggie Smith and Jonathan Kent has been immensely enjoyable; and I'm extremely grateful to them.

Christopher Hampton
March 2019

A German Life was first presented at the Bridge Theatre, London, on 6 April 2019. The cast was as follows:

Brunhilde Pomsel Maggie Smith

Director Jonathan Kent
Designer Anna Fleischle
Lighting Jon Clark
Sound Paul Groothuis
Design Associate Liam Bunster
Props Supervisors Marcus Hall Props
Costume Supervisor Eleanor Dolan

Character

Brunhilde Pomsel

A GERMAN LIFE

A suggestion of a quite small domestic kitchen in Munich. A plain table covered with a gingham cloth and a simple wooden chair on which, nursing a bowl of coffee, sits Brunhilde Pomsel, a compact woman with heavy black-rimmed glasses, a lined, craggy face and a confident air. She's 102, although there's nothing in her lively demeanour or obviously sharp intelligence to betray this fact.

As the lights come up, she acknowledges the audience, takes a sip of coffee and reflects for a moment.

Brunhilde Pomsel I've forgotten such a lot. Most of it, really. Certain things stick of course, although I've no idea why. I don't understand how it works. I read something and then I go across the room to check what's for dinner and completely forget what I've just read. I think, wait a minute, I've only just read that: I read it with my eyes wide open, I digested it – and now it's gone. And then, all of a sudden, things from long, long ago surge up into my mind. Things I can remember in the minutest detail.

She looks up at the audience.

So you'll have to . . . Anyway, let's see how we go.

Pause.

I can remember the outbreak of the First World War, that's probably as good a place to start as any. I was three, we were staying with my grandmother in the country and my father sent a telegram to say he'd been

3

called up, one of the very first batch. So we travelled back to Berlin and took a hansom cab, which was an unheard-of luxury, my mother, my baby brother and me, to the Potsdam station, to see him off. And I remember she bought pears, a bag of pears.

After that we didn't see much of my father, he was in Russia all through the war, although he must have come home on leave a few times, because by the end of the war there were five of us, I had four little brothers. When he came back we kept saying to each other who's this strange man in the flat? The first thing he did was he abolished the use of chamber-pots, so that if we had to get up in the middle of the night, we had to creep through the building in the dark, past all the witches and the evil spirits.

I suppose it was a happy childhood, whatever that means, God knows. They were always complaining about having no money, but we paid the rent and we never went hungry. My dad was a painter and decorator, so he was always in work, even during the inflation. He was very quiet, he never talked about his childhood, or the war, or anything very much. All the same, our whole world revolved around him. We were brought up very strictly, a clip round the ear or a thrashing with the carpet beater if you did anything wrong. And being the eldest and the only girl, everything was always my fault: you were there, why didn't you stop it happening? But all the same, it was fine, we were a normal German family. If you're crowded together in a small flat, love doesn't necessarily conquer all: no, the main thing is obedience – plus a few fibs and a bit of shifting the blame on to other people.

I was good at primary school and the teacher said to my mother: she's bright, she needs to stay in school. My mother started trying to squeeze the money out of my

4

dad, but then the teacher got the secondary school to give me a free place for a year and I moved up – but then I wasn't quite so good any more, geography, maths, chemistry, I couldn't do any of those; and my reports started saying 'Brunhilde's disruptive', 'Brunhilde never stops chattering in class' and so on. And I was hopeless at games, I was a clumsy little thing, I'd been wearing glasses since I was nine, I was terrified of ball-games and in the gym I'd get stuck on the horizontal bar and they'd have to help me down. What I wanted was to be an opera singer, like my friend Ilse's mother. I used to go round to help Ilse with her homework – her parents were very rich, there was always coffee and cake and her mother was Italian, they had a beautiful piano and she used to sing arias for us, *Carmen*, all sorts. But that was obviously out of the question. Or a hairdresser, I wouldn't have minded being a hairdresser, they get trips to Paris, any number of perks. But my father said: that's enough, I've paid out enough, out you come. So I left school when I was fifteen.

At first I was supposed to stay at home and help my mother with the housework, that was never going to go well. (*She laughs.*) It was a catastrophe. Especially in the kitchen, where I got everything wrong. So I looked in the paper and found this job they were advertising, secretary in a fashion house, Gläsinger and Co., in a very chic part of town, and I saw they were interviewing for it that very day. I jumped on the S-Bahn and just got there in time, a beautiful place, red carpet all the way up the stairs, I thought they'd throw me out right away. But no, I was interviewed by this severe-looking man with a white goatee, Herr Bernblum, yes, a Jew, pretty impenetrable, but he turned out to have quite a personality. And he said he'd take me on as a sort of trainee for the princely sum of 25 Marks a month, and I'd have to get my parents' permission as I was only sixteen. There was hell to pay when I got home – outrageous, where did I get the train fare, et cetera and so on: but finally Mother came in with me and we signed a two-year contract. I'd always wanted to work in an office. It was bliss.

The employees had to use the back entrance, which meant you had to come upstairs through Dispatch, the Sewing-room and the Pressing-room – and a wonderful room, always kept very warm, with thick carpets and gauzy curtains and the mannequins, or models I suppose you'd call them, running around in their smalls. Made coming to work a real experience. And I got all this training in the evenings: typing, basic book-keeping and shorthand, where I really hit the bullseye. I was determined to shine at that, because I was desperately in love with the instructor. Unrequited, needless to say, although he was very complimentary about the shorthand. I was great at it. Trust me to be best at something no one needs any more. I loved it there. I mean, sometimes Herr Bernblum would ask me to make tea for him, which I found a bit . . . you know, I wasn't the tea-lady, but otherwise I felt really at home there.

When the two years were up, they offered me a permanent position at 90 Marks a month. I had to get my parents' agreement as I was still under twenty-one – and my father said no, not enough, you have to demand 100. I said, but . . . and he said not a penny less than 100! So I told Herr Bernblum and he said, I'm sorry, in that case we're going to have to let you go. And they did. So I had to go to the labour exchange. It was 1929, the year of mass unemployment; and the jobs I was sent for were just the dregs. For example, there was a margarine factory up in the most sinister part of North Berlin, you could smell it three streets away. I just made an excuse, told them I had some sort of wasting disease. Finally, they sent me to a bookshop and I was offered a job right away at 100 a month. It was rather a . . . it was a Jewish business.

Very nice man, but he was hardly ever there. Otherwise there was an elderly clerk, an accounts lady who only ever ate bread and dripping and a repulsive youth who fortunately always arrived late. All I had to do was handle subscriptions, fill out forms and do bank transfers.

The winter of '29 was bitter, absolutely bitter, we weren't allowed to wear trousers or boots, tights hadn't been invented and the youth kept letting the stove go out. I kept thinking this isn't what I trained for, it was all so stupid and ugly.

Luckily, my father ran into a neighbour and ex-customer in the street, an insurance broker, Herr Dr Hugo Goldberg, my dad always had a few Jewish customers, he liked them, they always paid best. They chatted and he said, what's your Hilde up to? And my father said, you know, this and that. And Herr Goldberg said, you know what, one of my secretaries is getting married, why don't you send your daughter along, she always seemed like a smart girl, and maybe, maybe . . . So I went round the next day, said hello and curtsied; and he said you're very young, but why don't we give it a whirl? So he gave me a four-week trial. Complicated, the insurance business, but I fitted in, I did quite well. Dr Goldberg was up to all sorts of rackets, they did a lot of business with oil tankers from Constin . . . Constan . . . You know, Istanbul, and they had a system for fiddling the dates and they'd make a packet, you know how it works . . . (*She rubs thumb and forefingers together.*) Not that any of it came my way, no, I was back down to 90 a month.

Around that time, I met my first boyfriend, Heinz, at a tea-dance. His father owned a factory in Königsberg, a porcelain factory, lavatories, bidets, that sort of thing. Heinz had a bust-up with him, because he didn't want to take over the factory, he wanted to be a journalist. And his father said: all right, go, see how you get on in Berlin!

7

Pause. Her expression softens.

Berlin. At that time, it was such a marvellous city.

*Light change. Projections: a panorama of Berlin in the
early thirties, in stills and film.*

It had everything you can think of on offer, everything
that could possibly be important to people: theatres,
concerts, huge, beautiful cinemas, cabarets, a wonderful
zoo and ultra-fashionable restaurants, obviously too
expensive for mere mortals. A lot of it was for people
with money, rich Jews, there were plenty of them in
Berlin. My parents couldn't afford to go to the theatre:
but there were choirs, dance festivals, my dad's bowling
club . . . and we lived in a very quiet part of town. There
were hardly any cars on the streets, there were markets
where the food was fresher and cheaper – and there was
peace and harmony. I never saw a single demonstration,
all that sort of thing happened in other parts of the city.
And when my brothers put on their brown shirts, they'd
travel out of the area.

*As the projections end, Brunhilde is on her feet.
When the lights go up, there's a secretarial desk with
a typewriter, behind which she eventually sits.*

But I was telling you about Heinz. He was very poor. He
wrote articles for a magazine called *Motoring and Sport*.
I used to type them for him and improve them quite a bit
as well, if the truth be told. He wrote incomprehensible
pieces for something called, what was it, the League, the
'Militant League for German Culture', a Nazi
publication, as it turned out, although I had no idea of
that at the time. One day he dragged me along to that
huge stadium, the Sports Hall . . . no, the Sports Palace.
Turned out to be a crowd of men with BO, a lot of
hanging about, some terrible loud music and then this fat
man in uniform arrived: Goering. I'd never heard of him

and I must say he gave a completely uninteresting speech. I said to Heinz: don't you ever take me to anything like this again! And he didn't. Yes, he was a Nazi, finished up in the SS. But he never tried to talk politics to me, never said there's this new party which is going to free Germany from the Jews, nothing like that. I was a girl, you see, he thought I was far too stupid and immature, it never crossed his mind a woman could understand these things. God, nowadays, when I see some schoolgirl giving her opinions on TV, I think, what an unbelievable difference, makes me feel three times as old as I am.

Heinz had a friend, a flight lieutenant from the First World War who wanted to write his memoirs, but he was having trouble with his typewriter, he wasn't what you'd call a very bright spark. His name was Wulf Bley, and he was a really nice man with a terribly nice wife and little boy. Heinz suggested I could help him and he hired me to take dictation at a Mark an hour. He'd had a good war, he wore some kind of gold badge, didn't mean anything to me – and he'd joined the Nazi Party very early on, they liked him. It was a godsend, because after three very happy years with Herr Dr Goldberg, he'd called me in to say things weren't going so well for him and he'd have to ask me to work mornings only, on half-pay. So from then on, I had two jobs: Jew in the morning, Nazi in the afternoon.

Politics was never discussed at home. I mean, I don't think my mother even knew which way Dad voted. Or vice versa. But in 1932, I turned twenty-one and I was very excited about finally being able to vote. I've no idea who I actually voted for; but it was a lovely day, a Sunday, and there were banners and music and posters all over Berlin, forget the politics, it was fantastic . . . Yes, I suppose I must have voted Nazi, like everyone else.

I certainly didn't vote for the Nazis when they won, in 1933. But who did I vote for? Can't remember. I think

I probably voted Nationalist, I liked the colours on their banners, black, white and red. On January 30th, when Hitler was made Chancellor or something, on that famous evening, Heinz dragged me on a pilgrimage to the Brandenburg Gate, where Hitler stood in the window with all those people cheering and yelling, it was like a football match, and they all felt really pleased with themselves, because they'd taken part in a historical event.

Projection of 30 January 1933. Brunhilde raises her arm in the Nazi salute.

I was cheering as well. I admit it. Of course, I wasn't tactless enough to tell the poor Jews at the office that I'd been there. Not that I was taking any of it seriously. I couldn't have been less interested. But I went along with Heinz because I was young and in love and that was what was important to me. And I also went with him that day in Potsdam when Hitler shook hands with old Hindenburg in front of the church.

Projection.

I'd remember that, even if they weren't forever showing it on television. I never even asked Heinz, what is all this nonsense? I just wasn't interested. He never tried to convert me, but he noticed how stupid I was about these things – and a few months later, we broke up, he wrote me a letter, typewritten. At first, I was really unhappy, I didn't take it at all well. But my friend Eva, I had a very good friend called Eva Löwenthal, Jewish, said, you're well out of it, she'd never liked him much, and she laughed herself silly when I told her he'd taken me along to wave at Hitler. And in the end I coped with it pretty well. I finished with Dr Goldberg as well. He was always having these muttered conversations with his wife and getting lots of letters from abroad and then, thank God, they sold all their things and got out in '33 or '34.

So there it was: the Third Reich. Beautiful summer in 1933, I went swimming a lot. Then, out of the blue, as a reward for his support, the Nazis offered Herr Bley a job, dramaturg at the Deutches Theater, a job he was utterly unsuited for, but he abandoned his book, of which, by the way, I can't remember a single detail, and asked me if I'd join him at the theatre. There, he had me installed in an office and disappeared. I just sat around, I had absolutely nothing to do. I used to wander round and drop in on the other secretaries. I was there chatting one day, when the door opened and who should step in but every young girl's dream, Attila Hörbiger, who was at the theatre playing William Tell. I sprang to my feet and offered him my chair, but he said, no, he was just passing through, brought out his cigarette case and offered me one. So when my parents' friends said how's your daughter doing, they said, you know, she's being offered cigarettes by famous actors.

Anyway, Herr Bley, my prince of poets, was out of his depth at the theatre and one day he said, I've been talking to some people at the Radio, how would you like to work there? I was delighted, I said yes right away, so he arranged it all and then one day he said, you are in the Party, aren't you?

I've never told anyone this before.

No, I'm not, I said. Hmm, he said, job like this, might be a good idea. All right then, I said. And he said, I'll have to check if they're open for membership right now. Thing was, everyone was clamouring to get into the Party that year and the way it worked was they'd let in a few hundred and then they'd run out of membership cards and refused all applications for a time. I'd invited my Jewish friend, Eva, for coffee, she never had any money, we always knew we'd have to pay – so I told her, sorry, I can't today, I have to join the Party. That's all right, she said, I'll come with you. We went down to the local office and there was a queue of at least a hundred people. But it all went quite quickly; Eva sat on the wall outside and I joined up: 2 Marks a month, but the really painful thing was the 10 Mark admission fee. It cleaned me out, so that was it for the coffee. And do you know, not a single person ever asked me if I was a member of the Party; so I really needn't have bothered.

Of course, there was a great upheaval going on at the Broadcasting Corporation, because so many of the board members and the managing directors and the technical directors had been thrown out on the street or sent to concentration camps, Jews, I suppose; and a lot of their secretaries had gone with them. Anyway, before we knew it, Herr Bley was on the board of directors and I had a lovely office of my own in this beautiful modern building, Broadcasting House. I'm afraid he didn't last long there either. He was a nobody, really, he couldn't do anything. I'm sure he was a good pilot, but he was a bit stupid, to tell you the truth, really not very bright, they couldn't be doing with him; in four months he was gone and I never set eyes on him again. But it was thanks to him I'd found my favourite job; I stayed on, because I had a very good contract, I was earning more than 200 Marks a month, a really princely sum.

At first, it was like it was at the theatre: I had nothing much to do, because he wasn't doing anything. I used to stand at the window and look out at the street and there wasn't much going on there either. But on the first day, one of the other secretaries said, there's a very good canteen here, come and have lunch with us. And, yes, they had a really nice canteen in the basement and a wonderful roof garden as well. And I made friends there, lasting friendships. They're all dead now, of course, except for one, who's a year older than me and she's in an old folks' home with dementia, although she still looks good, not a day older than 65. Eventually, they put me in the press department, where I covered the opening of the big broadcasting exhibition, and that's where they found out how good my shorthand was, when I took down a speech, funnily enough by Goebbels, who came to open the exhibition. So I was a big success in the press department.

I can't remember quite why now, but later on I landed up in Current Events. That was the best time of my life. All those wonderful men. The reporters. News and sport, they really worked us. We met every morning early over coffee and cakes and then they sent out the radio cars – the Echo cars they were called – to do the outside broadcasts, then rush the recordings back to the studio. We covered all kinds of things, foreign visitors, football matches, premieres, financial stories. All over the city. Everything had to be done incredibly fast. There was a lot of stress, not that the word had been invented in those days. And no regular hours or breaks: but at the end of the day, we'd all get together for a drink and usually a meal at our regular corner-house. A lot of them had cars, so I could usually rely on a lift home. We all had such a good time.

Yes, Germany was wonderful in those years leading up to the Olympic Games.

Projections: scenes from the Berlin Olympic Games, 1936: Hitler, Goebbels, Jesse Owens.

Berlin came alive, it was transformed into the most beautiful, well-ordered, civilised city, you could have been in Paris. And that amazing new stadium; it was every bit as good as the Games we had here in Munich in 1972. The best thing was all these foreigners finally coming back to Germany: not only the Europeans, but all sorts of exotic creatures. I can't remember seeing any blacks, although I did see one once in the zoo, at the zoo, I mean. But all sorts of people with different coloured skins, someone I had to show round Broadcasting House, can't remember if he was an Indian or a Japanese, anyway someone from a completely different world, he caused quite a sensation. Everyone took paying guests, we even managed to squeeze three large Dutch people into our little flat. I didn't actually see much of the Games themselves, tickets were hard to get and they were expensive, all I could manage was a ticket for the dressage, is that what it's called? Anyway, the whole thing was a great experience. And the Dutch people sent us presents from Holland, biscuits, you know, and cheese.

It's true, you simply had to admit it, so many things suddenly got better when Hitler came in, so many young people felt . . . liberated. And there was no persecution of the Jews, everything was fine. I mean . . . well, that's to say, obviously, there was boycotting of Jewish businesses, I remember that. Even in our quiet suburb.

My father's Jewish clientele, and . . . as I said, I worked for Herr Dr Goldberg for four years . . . and I did notice, in 1933, something was going on. And he, he didn't, didn't stay in, in, erm, in Berlin, I'm trying to say. Or in Germany, as far as I knew. I mean, you did read in the paper that a lot of Jews were emigrating. But you didn't associate that with . . . anything terrible. That's when we heard about concentration camps for the first time. People who spoke against the government or started riots were sent there for re-education. Re-education, you see, nobody gave it a second thought. Then our top announcer, Jule Jänisch, a wonderful man, one of the founders of the Broadcasting Corporation, who read the news morning, noon and night, was suddenly in the concentration camp. Why? Well, it turns out he was queer. He was a queer, for

God's sake! Such a nice, friendly man. Oh, yes, friendly enough, people said, but he was queer. We didn't even know what that meant, couldn't begin to imagine. We really were an inhibited bunch.

Anyway, quite suddenly, Rosa Lehmann Oppenheimer, who used to do our laundry – her little shop was suddenly gone. And so was she. Hordes of Germans arrived, who'd been thrown out of Poland and Czechoslovakia, all their villages were deserted; and we were told all the Jews from here had been sent to replace them. And little by little, Rosa and Dr Goldberg and Herr Levi, our neighbour, whose daughter Hilde I'd grown up with, and all Dad's customers disappeared. Until that terrible thing in November, what the hell was it called, the famous night when they broke all the glass – yes, Kristallnacht. Kristallnacht . . . I'm sorry, I've lost my thread.

Silence.

Eva. Eva Löwenthal.

Pause.

She was a real Jew. I knew her parents, you couldn't get more Jewish. She didn't *look* that Jewish, she was very pretty, beautiful eyes, not very tall, reddish hair, very delicate features, but she did have that Jewish . . .

She describes with her finger the shape of a hooked nose.

She often used to come and visit me at Broadcasting House, she had no money and she used to go on these long walks through Berlin and finish up in my office. My men, the reporters, all liked her enormously because she was incredibly clever and witty, she made them all laugh. Sometimes someone would say, she's a little Jewess, isn't she, and I'd say, I think so, yes, something along those lines. She was so well-read and clever, she often used to make me feel really stupid. I'd had such a rudimentary education and she knew everything. But we were all aware she needed protection: for one thing she had no money. I remember going to visit her once when she was ill in bed and there was no furniture in her family's little flat, just a table and a few chairs. She made her living writing for the magazines – not the Nazi press, obviously (*She laughs.*) – but the more liberal papers; she was a very talented columnist, but she'd only get an article published once every couple of months or so, she clearly didn't earn enough to support the family, leave alone the fact she'd rather spend it on cigarettes than food. Eventually, they had to move further out, Eva, her parents and her sister, who was selling vacuum cleaners from door to door, and they all had to live in one room. Dreadful. Eva had been ordered to do manual labour for the city, which she refused to do. So all their welfare payments had been stopped.

What could you do? Nothing. I mean, I suppose I could have travelled out every day and helped them. But she had other friends and we all agreed: there was nothing we could do to help. Especially if she preferred to see the little money she had going up in smoke, rather than buying food with it. I don't mean to be judgemental, it's just a detail, I'm just trying to give you a clear picture.

Nowadays, people like to think they'd have done more for the poor persecuted Jews. And I'm sure when they say that, they mean it sincerely. But they wouldn't have. Everyone had too many problems of their own to worry about the Jews. It was as if the whole country was under a bell-jar. Germany was one gigantic concentration camp.

Not that that excuses anything.

She sighs. Long pause.

I remember the day war was declared, I remember it vividly. I can see myself standing in the office and the announcement coming over the loudspeakers. Everyone was very upset, there was no cheering or anything, people were genuinely upset. And very soon, one by one, our reporters started to disappear – to Poland, to Russia, even to Africa. My friend, Otti Kreppke, he was a football reporter, they gave him all the second division games, and he was sent to Africa and never came back. He was a very close friend, I could have married him. A year or so later, when we took France, some of the older reporters were sent to Paris, where they had a great time. And they'd always bring back something nice, a bottle of cognac, a chic pair of gloves, once one of them brought me a fantastic hat. The rest of us had rationing – on clothes and food. I didn't eat sausage, I only liked cheese and I remember my mother saying, oh, my God, what am I going to put in Brunhilde's sandwiches? Luckily, because I'd had TB, I got supplementary coupons for butter and full-fat milk, also for meat, which were instantly ripped out of my hand. And we were all remarkably relaxed about the war, which in any case was going extremely well. Until those pages and pages of casualties started appearing in the papers. That gave us pause for thought.

Montage: images from the early days of the war, reflecting all the German triumphs. When the lights are reset, Brunhilde is in a different, more luxurious office.

As the Broadcasting House staff thinned out, we suddenly had a new Director-General from Cologne, Glasmeier, very nice man. But he brought in all his people from Cologne and gave them all the plum jobs. And it just stopped being fun, working at the Corporation. Our personnel department did a lot of work with the

Propaganda Ministry and one day they needed a shorthand-typist. I was well known for my shorthand, so they asked me to go and see Herr Feige, the deputy head. He interviewed me and then he said, right, good, there'll be a desk for you here starting Monday. I said I can't, I'm in the middle of a lot of things at Broadcasting House, I have to clear my office and everything; and he said, I don't think you're listening to me, you're to be here Monday morning, nine o'clock.

I was told I was to be the secretary to Dr Naumann, he was in the SS, he was Goebbels's deputy, but he took one look at me and said, I'm not having her in my office, she looks like a Jew. So I was passed on to a Herr Frowein, one of Goebbels's personal assistants. I got on very well with him. He was a young officer who'd been slightly wounded, married, expecting their first baby. He was one of, I think, four personal assistants to Goebbels, they did three-day shifts, during which they had to stick to him as closely as his shadow. When he went to the lavatory, they had to be there. Wherever he went, his houses, his properties, when he met people, when he ate, they had to be with him and they had to sleep nearby, wherever he finished up. They had to stay so stuck to him, they were known as Goebbels's underpants.

Goebbels, yes . . .

She breaks off and reflects for a moment.

When he walked into the office, we all had to stand up and stay standing till he'd left. The first time he came in, I thought to myself, he's good-looking, he's damned good-looking, and he was, especially when he was out of uniform, he was unusually well turned-out, so many of them were hooligans, but he wore the most beautiful suits, very well-cut, and he was always lightly tanned; I think he must have had a manicure every day.

*Projection: Goebbels, in a trench-coat, advances
between crowds of supporters, held back by the SA.
He walks with a very noticeable limp.*

He was quite short, of course, not tall enough to be
genuinely impressive; and the foot thing, there was no
way to hide that. Everyone said he was very charming,
but he wasn't to us, because he didn't need to be, we
were just part of the furniture; he was perfectly friendly,
but he never smiled at anybody. Never unpleasant. Just
neutral. He dealt with whatever needed to be dealt with,
said 'Heil Hitler' and left. Sometimes, when I was doing
the Sunday shift, a couple of his children would arrive
with Tell, their big Airedale, to collect him and walk back
with him to their town house by the Brandenburg Gate.
Lovely children, very well brought-up. No older than six
or seven. They loved it if you let them have a go on the
typewriter. I'd sit them at the desk, put in a sheet of paper
and say, now write a letter to Daddy. They loved that.

I'd have liked to have had children, but it wasn't to be.

Anyway, it wasn't long before I saw a different side of
him. Two of us were told to go and listen to his speech
in the Sports Palace. I was the most recently arrived and
Fräulein Deckmann was the youngest, so we drew the
short straws. An SS man put us into a very chic Mercedes,
which was a good start; we were given excellent seats,
close to the speaker's podium. The place was packed full
of factory workers, none of whom, I may say, were there
voluntarily. Frau Goebbels and a couple of their children
were sitting right behind us. We'd only just arrived and
off they went. The usual martial music and all that
business. And then Goebbels was on.

*Sound cue: Goebbels's 'Total War' speech, his voice
rising to a feverish crescendo.*

I'd never experienced anything like it in my life. He managed to work himself up into such a state, I don't think he even knew himself what he was saying. I can't, I don't know how to describe the way he succeeded in bringing hundreds of people to their feet as if they'd been stung by a wasp, shouting and chanting and rejoicing, but he did succeed. Little Fräulein Deckmann and I were paralysed, clutching on to each other's hands, when the SS man tapped us on the shoulder and said, well, girls, applaud, at least you can applaud: so we did. A bit. Otherwise they'd have lynched us. But we were appalled. We could hardly breathe, we were so frightened. That one man had the power to get that huge crowd to yell, yes, we want total war, over and over again, you wanted to shake your head and say, what, are they all drunk? But they had no choice. They had lost their individuality. They were bewitched by this tiny man. It was like, I don't know, Jesus or something.

Projection: colour film of the speech, Goebbels's brown uniform against the red banners, the hysteria of the crowd.

You have to admit, Goebbels was a wonderful actor . . . well, a good actor, let's say. It was an actor's transformation: this quiet, elegant, serious man we saw in the office, transformed into a demented midget.

Pause. She reflects for a moment.

Only once it happened in the office: some man came to visit and we suddenly heard Goebbels screaming his head off. We all turned to stone. One of the older secretaries said, well, *this* has never happened before. We couldn't believe it – and it never happened again. Otherwise he was always a model of restraint.

Pause.

I'm often asked what exactly I was doing in the Propaganda Ministry, what kind of things would come across my desk and I always have to say, my dear, young people, how should I know, we're talking about more than sixty years ago, so I have no idea, I can't remember. It wasn't very interesting, that I can tell you; I certainly didn't attach any importance to it. The job wasn't much fun, it wasn't the kind of work, where you'd go home in the evening and say: I did well, that was a really satisfying day. You went in, you sat there, you typed something, somebody blathered away at you on the telephone. You were only allowed to use blue ink, green ink was for the Minister and red ink was for the Private Secretary. You were supposed to multiply the dreadful atrocities of the enemy, so if the agency report said, twenty women were raped by the Russians in some village, you had to say it was thirty. And they used to say, over and over again, unlike the press in the past, which falsified everything, you can trust us, we alone will tell you the truth. Of course, we secretaries never saw any of the really important papers. Sophie Scholl and her brother, for instance, who were guillotined, we heard nothing about that. In fact, one day, Herr Frowein handed me the whole file about them and the movement they tried to start, the White Rose, and said, put that in the safe, would you, but don't look at it. He was half joking, but of course, I did what he said, even though he left me alone with that file and, God, I really wanted to look at it. I felt ever so proud of myself. Still do, actually. They were idealists, those kids, thought of themselves as resistance fighters, got caught right away, it was stupid of them, really. If they'd kept their mouths shut, they might still be alive. Those poor kids, what they did to them, just because of some shitty leaflet . . .

She breaks off; for a moment she almost seems about to burst into tears; then she recovers.

The atmosphere changed after Stalingrad. Obviously they tried to play it down and pretend it made no difference, the nice office with the beautiful furniture was still there, but there was a definite crack in the façade, things tightened up. There were more restrictions and punishments. There was a cinema in the ministry and we were made to watch things like that general on trial, having to hold up his trousers because they'd taken away his belt and being yelled at and humiliated by the judge, as if he was a common criminal. I can still see those images.

Projection: Judge Roland Freisler rants at the defendants in the Stauffenberg trial.

All those horrors we know about now, we didn't know about them at the time. Very few people did. Just those who came into direct contact with what was going on. And they kept quiet about it. I suppose there were some people who listened to the BBC, but you could be executed for that, and no one would have confided in me, because they knew I worked for Goebbels and kept their mouths shut when I was around. I remember running into Eva on the bus and she said it's time I paid another visit on you and your nice men; and I had to explain to her I wasn't at Broadcasting House any more, I'd been transferred to the Propaganda Ministry and I was working for Goebbels: oh, my God, she said, well, that's the last you'll see of me. And it was.

Pause.

I suppose the truth is, we didn't really want to know. All we knew was that the war was terrible and that the whole world was against us. And even people who had friends or family living abroad . . . I've forgotten what I was going to say.

Silence.

Oh yes, Goebbels. I remember the time he and his wife visited the Venice Biennale.

Projection: Goebbels in St Mark's Square.

And he happened to say how much he was missing his dog, Tell. So some poor press attaché was ordered to take the dog with him when he flew down to give the Minister the daily briefing. He tried to refuse, but when he got to the airport, there was the dog. Flying a dog to Venice in the middle of the war! Needless to say, Goebbels went berserk, are you insane, what idiot is responsible for this, don't you know how sensitive he is, it'll take him months to recover from this, take him back, now! That was one of the favourite stories going round the office.

To tell you the truth, I hardly knew Goebbels. So I was delighted when he invited me to dinner at his house together with one of the other secretaries. I was looking forward to getting to know Frau Goebbels and see the children, but as luck would have it, they were away at one of their villas or castles or whatever. I'd heard she was always the life and soul of the party – but she wasn't there, and actually I never did meet her. There were about twenty of us for dinner, mostly Gauleiters and people, and I discovered, with great trepidation, that I was sitting next to Goebbels, on his right. I thought of a whole lot of things to say to him, that my brothers were all at the front, that my father was a First World War veteran who'd joined the Home Guard: but as it turned out, he didn't say a single word to me the whole evening, not even to ask if I was enjoying the goose. He just held forth about how his favourite hotel, the Kaiserhof, which was so much better than the Bristol or the Adlon, had been totally destroyed in the bombing. We'd been told to stop eating when he did and it turned out he ate incredibly fast, it was a job to keep up with him. Then he scoffed some kind of pudding, leapt to his feet and led us into the film room, where coffee was served and we had to watch some utterly stupid, boring American comedy. And as the lights went up, there were our SS men to whisk us away, back to the office.

That was what he was like. Completely impersonal. One night, on his birthday, we all went to the theatre and I was designated to sit next to him. He never said a word to me then, either. He was said to be very fond of women, but that meant actresses and models, not secretaries. A lot of them used to come in and see him, he used to make all the casting decisions for the big films. It was his hobby, that's how he relaxed. There were jokes about it in the office. At the top of the Propaganda Ministry he had a lovely little flat with its own private entrance, and if we were working late and there was an air raid, we used to have to go up, open all the windows, pull down the blackout blinds and fill the bathtub, which was so huge it took half an hour to fill. It was very elegantly furnished, an enormous pink bed, I believe it was pink, in the bedroom, where I suppose many a love scene was played with various actresses; there was one in particular, Lida Baarová, a Czech, I think, yes, lot of jokes about invading Czechoslovakia, he was madly in love with her, and wanted to leave his family for her. Of course, Hitler couldn't allow the perfect German family with the six blond children to be broken up, so he intervened and had her sent away, back to Czechoslovakia. Goebbels was supposed to have wept when it happened and I believe it; he must have thought, God in Heaven, why can't I give up all this politics shit and just live with this beautiful woman? I can imagine he might have thought that way, if only for a minute.

Anyway, film was his real enthusiasm and any film that looked as if it might be successful, he would get himself involved with. For instance, that historical film where

Ferdinand Marian was forced to play a Jew, *Jew Süss*,
I think it was called. Marvellous film, and he was
wonderful. He didn't want to act in it, but they made
him. They probably said, you want to be in a film or you
want to be in a concentration camp? It was an enormous
success. And there was another one, *Kolberg*, the last one
Goebbels made. Huge battle scenes, otherwise I can't
remember much about it. It was right towards the end of
the war and they brought thousands of soldiers back from
the front to be extras. Of course, it was very optimistic in
tone. The Germans won.

She laughs.

I almost finished up working in the film industry myself.
As I said, I liked my boss, Herr Frowein, very much. He
was very reserved – and after a while, I worked out why.
It was because, far from being a Nazi, he found the whole
business utterly atrocious; he tried to avoid sticking his
arm up in the air whenever possible and as he knew I
wasn't a tart for Hitler either, we had a kind of complicity.
Not that he ever said anything, but his expression would
often speak volumes. I think he rather exaggerated the
seriousness of his wound for the very good reason that he
didn't want to get sent back to the Eastern Front. Not
that he need have worried, because Goebbels suddenly
fired the head of the Film Department, Herr Hilpert, for
persistent drunkenness or something and appointed him
instead. So he came to me and said, well, Pomseline, how
about coming out to Babelsberg with me? I was ecstatic,
but then the next day Herr Frowein said, I'm really sorry,
Naumann says it's out of the question, we're not giving her
away. And so I found myself working for Herr Naumann,
who'd obviously forgotten he thought I looked like a Jew.
Made me miserable, but, you know, I was very dutiful.
And what with all the ministerial bonuses and whatnot,
I was making the best part of 500 a month. Just insane.

Projection: bombs falling on Berlin.

I'd been at a party, the summer of '43 this was, some
birthday party or something, and I got home just before
midnight, you know, on the last train. My parents were
away, staying with friends. I was wearing a little silk
cocktail dress, French, I knew a little woman who had
connections in France, who made them for me. Anyway,
suddenly the sirens went off, so it was down to the
shelter before I'd had a chance to change. I grabbed my
sewing-basket, it was full of stockings, stockings were
in short supply and I was very good at fixing ladders, so
all my friends used to give me theirs and I'd repair them
with this little wooden contraption, it's what I did to pass
the time during the air raids. This raid was by far the
worst there'd ever been, terrifying. It was so loud and it
went on for so long. For a minute, we thought we were
done for. When it had eased off a bit, our air-raid
warden, a terribly nice woman, went to investigate. A
minute later, she came back and said, the roof's on fire.
She called everybody out to help, but there was nothing
to be done, and it was starting to spread down the walls.

Our flat was on the upper ground floor and I thought
I could just quickly check it. There was quite a lot of
damage from the blast. The big mirror in my bedroom
was shattered. The budgie was still alive but . . . I can see
him now, but I had to leave him behind. I just grabbed
the next month's ration cards for me and my parents
from the kitchen table, stuffed them in my handbag and
ran back down. That's when I noticed the houses on the
other side of the street had completely disappeared and
we were surrounded by a wall of fire. Luckily, some
firemen had arrived: they wrapped us in soaking wet
blankets and literally dragged us through the flames.
I came out the other side still clutching that damned
basket of stockings, although, would you believe it, my
handbag – with the ration cards – was gone. Disaster.

Like losing your passport today. It was dreadful, but somehow, with one side of your brain you thought, no food for a month, and with the other side you thought, heigh ho, now what? And I found some other big shelter and even managed to get some sleep.

The next morning, there were announcements over the loudspeakers telling us to go to the park, where they gave us – hundreds of us – coffee and rolls. I wasn't sure what to do next, everything around where I lived was a pile of rubble, so I thought, the only thing to do is head for my office. No transport, of course, there was nothing on the roads, the only thing for it was to walk. It was a hot day and on the way I passed a couple of workmen and one said: oo, look, she's growing radishes on her toes, because I had red polish on my toenails. I thought, you arsehole, the night I've been through and all you can do is make stupid jokes. Funny, the things you can't remember and the things you'll never forget. Anyway, at the office, at first everybody laughed when I arrived in my party frock and red sandals, but when they understood what had happened, they couldn't have been nicer. Frau Goebbels's private secretary happened to be in the office that day, and she went and told her that a girl on the staff had been bombed out and was standing there in a cocktail dress. Good heavens, Frau Goebbels said, we can't have that, and do you know, she fetched out of her own wardrobe a lovely dark-blue suit, lined in white silk. Of course she was twice my size, so I looked ridiculous, but I had it altered the next day and I've never had such a beautiful suit, the most wonderful fine wool. I wore it a lot. It outlived its owner. It's what I was wearing when I came out of prison.

Pause.

As the war was coming to an end, some of us used to work in Goebbels's private house in Hermann-Goering-Strasse, don't suppose they call it that any more. The weather was lovely, so I was working outside on the terrace there, when one of his assistants, a Dr Collatz, came over and said, I've requisitioned a motorbike to go over to Potsdam. My wife and daughter are out there. I want to say goodbye to them, you know, I want to see them again. Aren't your parents somewhere near there, Fräulein Pomsel? Would you like me to give you a lift? I jumped at the chance. He dropped me off and said he would collect me at seven to take me back. Well, by nine o'clock there was no sign of him and my mother said, that's good, you stay here with us, my girl. But I thought that would be, I don't know, desertion, so the next morning I got up at six and went to the station and a train arrived. Where it came from I've no idea, turned out no trains were expected to run that day, but anyway, there it was, I got on it like a fool. On the way I heard the Brandenburg Gate was being shelled by the Russians, so when I got there, I ran like hell, straight into the Ministry's air-raid shelter, where I spent the next two weeks. Meanwhile, Dr Collatz had taken his wife and ten-year-old daughter, who was slightly handicapped, down to the lake shore, where he shot them and then himself.

Pause.

Of course, we were used to people dying and being killed.

The strange thing was he hadn't said anything to me, but I suppose he thought, she's clever enough to take a hint. It would never have crossed his mind I'd be stupid enough to slog my way back to the Ministry. It was really stupid of me. My trouble was I was always too conscientious. Anybody with any sense would've known the war was lost, but . . . it's so hard to think yourself back into the state of mind you were in at the time. Numb. Paralysed. I think that's probably the best word. And a few years later, you say to yourself, did I really think those things

28

or is it only now I think I thought them? Sorry, but it's all quite complicated.

You see, there was this thing called the Wenck army out there somewhere and it was supposed to circle round the Russians and attack them from behind – and there were a few idiots who believed that was actually going to happen: including me. The bloody Wenck army and the secret miracle weapons, the new rockets, they were supposed to turn everything around. I was so stupid; I believed that almost up to the last day. I simply couldn't imagine that we might lose the war. The Propaganda Ministry certainly worked on me.

Anyway, there we sat, in that hideous shelter, like mice in a trap. Diet was a bit eccentric, everything came out of cans. I remember a couple of days when we ate nothing but tins and tins of asparagus, pounds of the stuff. And luckily, there was plenty of drink, wine, all sorts, so everyone was permanently slightly pickled, we needed an anaesthetic. There was absolutely nothing to do, no work, nothing. It wasn't even worth thinking any more, there was no point. It was all over. We'd been there about ten days, when Goebbels's adjutant, a Lieutenant Schwägermann, very nice man, came over from the Führer's bunker, which was across the courtyard. He told us Hitler had committed suicide. Well, we all knew what that meant. End of the war.

I have no memory of what happened then, but the following evening, Schwägermann came back and said Goebbels had committed suicide. Somehow we were more affected by that news. His wife as well, he told us. What about the children? The children as well. After that, no one could speak.

> *She puts her hands in front of her eyes. Deep breath.*
> *As she resumes, a projection: the six Goebbels children*
> *in various home movies.*

Inconceivable. Why would they do that? There was a plane standing by to fly them out of Berlin. The thing I'll never understand is the attitude of the mother. Unforgivable. How can a mother kill the children she's brought into the world? Why couldn't they have lived to become their own people? Premeditated murder, as big a crime as anything that happened all through the war. All very well for those cowards to blow their brains out or crunch their cyanide pills, but why kill those children? Apparently, the eldest sensed something was wrong and struggled as hard as she could against taking the pill. They had to call the doctor to hold her down. (*She shakes her head.*) It's impossible to imagine.

She takes a moment to recover.

You know, there was no Propaganda Ministry before the war – and there's been no Propaganda Ministry since. (*She laughs.*) And do we miss it? It was nothing to do with idealism or love of the Fatherland. It was just a means of exercising control and falsifying the news, it was sheer egotism on the part of those crazy Nazis.

Not that I realised any of this at the time.

Goebbels had been the Gauleiter of Berlin, and it was his deputy, a nice man called Hans Fritzsche who appeared next and told us that, as Gauleiter, it was his task to surrender to the Russians, so he needed a white flag. There were a lot of sacks of flour and rice and noodles in the shelter, so he had us empty them out to make a huge flag about this big.

She stretches out her arms to indicate the size of the flag.

We had no means of sewing them, but we managed to cobble them together somehow. As we were doing this, we noticed the sounds of the war were gradually dying away. No more artillery, just very occasional small-arms fire. Anyway, when the flag was finished, Fritzsche and a few others set off to find the Russians, telling us to stay where we were and promising they'd look out for us. Well, we sat there for hours; we were just starting to think he'd left us in the lurch, when a troop of armed Russian soldiers suddenly burst in, they looked like Mongolians, all slant-eyed. They herded us together and marched us out the back door into the open air, shoving us out with their guns. We were terrified, I'm telling you, we all thought the end was nigh. We looked pretty green and cadaverous by then and they were leading us away from the Ministry, when, miraculously, we bumped into Herr Fritzsche and his flag, very ragged by now, but recognisable; and he and his people were with another squad of Russians, with much better groomed officers, who yelled at the Mongolians, who made themselves scarce. Later, I was told they'd been shot, but I don't suppose that can be true. In any case, God knows whether they'd been planning to rape us or kill us, so we probably had a really lucky escape. Then, we were taken to Russian Military HQ and were handed over to agents in good suits, working directly for the Russian commandant in Berlin, Hotschin or Hutschik or Chuikov or whatever he was called. By now, we were being shuffled about like chess pieces and in the end, we were marched all the way to the airport, down Leipziger-strasse, past a lot of dead horses and tripping over human corpses.

Projection: aerial shots of the ruins of Berlin at the end of the war.

We spent the night, ten of us crammed into two small rooms near the airport, no food, nothing to drink; and then we were interrogated, in great detail, one by one. There was a lot of discussion about what to say so as not to contradict one another: some people thought they'd say they'd just stepped into the shelter to get away from the shooting and had nothing to do with the Propaganda Ministry, others said that wasn't a good idea, a lot of squabbling. I decided I was going to tell the truth. More or less. So I said I was just a typist for that dreadful Dr Goebbels, that the offices were so extensive, I'd never even clapped eyes on him. I thought I did rather well and they were very polite and the interpreters seemed to know what they were doing. To be honest, at that stage, I was so done in, I wouldn't have cared if they'd taken me out and shot me, I felt dead inside. But they were so civilised and friendly I started to think maybe I'll be home in time for Dad's birthday on May the 7th. I can bake him a cake. (*She smiles ruefully.*) I thought, the war's over, everything should go back to normal. After the interrogation, they thanked me nicely, I was led away . . . and I didn't get out for five years.

Buchenwald wasn't so bad.

1945 was a beautiful summer and we sunned ourselves in front of the barracks, sitting around with nothing to do, chatting. I remember saying, God knows what the conditions are like back home, at least here in the Soviet hotel we get our pearl barley soup three times a day. And they had a theatre in Buchenwald with a proper stage and an orchestra pit and quite a few musicians from the Philharmonic. The Russians provided instruments and we had wonderful concerts. And they had sort of circus shows, people pouring buckets of water over each other, that sort of thing. Later, I was transferred to Sachsenhausen and they had proper theatre people there; and the commandant allowed this play to be rehearsed. Then one of the actresses got caught with a Russian soldier; he got sent back to Russia and she was dismissed from the play. There was a week to go before the opening and somebody said, you used to work in the radio, didn't you, why don't you play the part, if you can learn the lines? So I did.

One of the questions the Russian interrogator asked me was whether or not I'd ever been issued with a cyanide pill. I said no: if anyone had offered me one, I'd have accepted, but not for me, I had no plans to do away with myself. Although I might have done towards the end of my time in prison, when I felt I was running out of steam. I got hold of a knife, which you weren't supposed to have, but it was really blunt. I remember thinking, how am I going to slit my wrists with a knife this blunt? It'd be more of a dent than a cut. Not a very reliable way to die. So I thought: stop all this rubbish and pull yourself together. This is no time to throw in the towel. And three months later, I was out.

I came out of prison in January 1950. I arrived home, put 24 Marks on the table and said, here you are, Mum, this is what I've earned in the last five years. My mother picked up the money and dropped it in the waste-paper basket. That's East German cash, she said, it doesn't work here. I found the world had completely changed: new currency, the DDR, the Nuremberg trials. And – I know people find this impossible to believe – the whole business with the Jews, the first I heard of it was when I got back from prison. Obviously, I'd always known there were concentration camps, but . . . but I had no idea they gassed and burned people there. And, you know, I'd been in Buchenwald standing under those showers. You had your hook, mine was number 47, you hung up your clothes, you had about a quarter of an hour in a big, tiled room, small piece of soap, nice warm water, until it suddenly ran cold – brrr – then you went into another room and your clothes had been cleaned and hung up on a different hook number 47. We really used to look forward to it, it only happened maybe twice a year; but now, looking back on it, it makes me feel ill, the thought that those same shower-heads were used to pump through gas, or whatever they did, to kill Jews.

Silence.

All those terrible things. We didn't *want* to know about them, we really didn't. I sat at my desk in the Propaganda Ministry and I knew as much or as little as the local greengrocer.

Pause.

Only a few years ago, when they built that memorial place, the Holocaust Information Centre, I went along and asked the man if he could give me information about a missing person. Yes, he said, if you have some details; and he took me to their computer. What's the name, he said, and I said, Löwenthal. Oh, that's quite a common Jewish name, he said, we have dozens of them, what's the first name? Eva, I said. Well, they had six Eva Löwenthals, at least. Only one was the right age, though. She'd been taken to Auschwitz in 1943 and she'd died in January 1945. That was all the information we could find. She was gone. And so were all the other Löwenthals.

She sits for a moment, playing with the thin chain she wears around her neck. Then she speaks with some vehemence.

I haven't learned very much in life, but one thing I do know: there is no such thing as justice. It doesn't exist. Not even within the legal system. Especially within the legal system. And I don't know whether God exists, probably not, but what certainly does exist is evil. And there's no justice.

I don't know what you think, but I don't believe I did anything wrong. Why should I feel guilty? I don't. How can you feel guilty for something you know nothing about? Yes, I worked in the Propaganda Ministry, but I wasn't given a choice. So I feel no guilt. On the contrary, I feel I was very unfairly treated by the Russians. All I did was type stuff for Goebbels. I had no idea what was going on. Or very little. No more than most people. So you can't make me feel guilty. Nor do I buy all that crap about the guilt of the German people. We were guilty of stupidity, I'll give you that, people were stupid and superficial, for instance when I was young I thought, why do I need to be interested in politics, I'm a woman. But how are you going to be able to prevent people thinking that way? Stupid people follow false leaders – and then they and all the rest of us have to pay the bill. More than anything else, people don't care. They watch all the dreadful things happening in Syria, then they switch off the TV and go out to dinner. Mind you, nowadays, I don't think people would be stupid enough to fall for the kind of nonsense we fell for. All that hot air, I don't think you can get that past people any more.

Long silence.

I moved into the home, what, only a couple of years ago. I pretty much keep myself to myself. The meals are communal, but I prefer to have them in my room: I mean, who wants to eat with a lot of old people? I've spent plenty of time on my own, but I've never really been lonely. As I said, I would have liked to have a family, but . . .

She breaks off.

Round about the time of the Olympic Games, I met a man in a café all of us from the radio used to go to. His name was Gottfried Kirchbach and I fell in love with him. He was twice my age. And he was married, with two daughters from a previous marriage. And he was Jewish – half-Jewish, actually, but the Nazis weren't that fussy. He was quite a well-known artist, painted a very successful series of political posters for the Social Democrats, which made the Nazis like him even less.

At the end of the year, he relocated to Amsterdam, where I used to visit him at weekends. It was quite complicated, what with his wife and his other girlfriends, but he made me very happy. When I got pregnant, I asked him if I could come to Amsterdam as well and have the baby there. But he didn't want that. In those days, you couldn't really have a child without being married, there was a lot of shame attached, which I didn't have the courage to face. Because I'd had TB, my doctor told me I was entitled to an abortion for health reasons: so that's what . . .

She breaks off, plays with the chain around her neck for a moment, pulls herself together.

I've never minded being on my own.

Gottfried had two more daughters with somebody else and then, in 1942, luckily for him, he dropped dead one day. The Nazis never got him.

Pause.

I don't know, how did I get to be so old? I'm such a miserable, frail creature; I can't see properly and I can't walk much, because I can't see. There doesn't seem to be any end to it. My pulse is regular, there's nothing wrong with my heart. I'm probably just not going to wake up one day. Yes, not an illness, I can't envisage that: in my sleep.

She laughs.

To tell you the truth, I couldn't care less. As long as I'm able to go on having these nice conversations with you.

She smiles bravely. Slow fade to black.